Simple Start-Up

How to Start a Home-Based Business.
Simply.

Jennifer Chase

Founder & CEO, Frugi Home Organizer, LLC.

ISBN-10: 1534648615
ISBN-13: 978-1534648616

DEDICATION

To anyone who has ever wanted to start a Home-Based Business.
Failed.
And then tried again.

CONTENTS

1   No Debt

2   No Inventory

3   No Pyramid

4   A Starter Kit that really gets you started

5   A Mission Statement that works

FRUGI HOME ORGANIZER, LLC.

MISSION STATEMENT

We are going to make money and live debt free
By helping others get organized and live burden free
So that all of us can be successful and live completely free

NO DEBT

You cannot start a business with debt. Listen! This is the best advice you will ever get! This can make you or break you! If you want to build a strong, firm, solid foundation in your Home-Based business or Brick and Mortar business or any type of business, you can't start your business with debt, owing someone else. If you begin and try to operate any business with debt, your chances of success are completely limited because your budget and flexibility become limited. You become a slave to the lender. You become a slave to lending companies, credit card companies, banks, and any one personally you owe money to. And that doesn't even include the interest!

I know we have all been taught to focus on our credit scores and live and die by those scores so that we can borrow debt to build more debt to pay off more debt to then go back into debt. It is a system and a constant hamster wheel that does not work. How many times have you said that you would pay off something you purchased on credit and didn't? How many times have you paid almost double for something because of the interest? How many times have you begun a business purchasing inventory, only to not sell it, then be stuck with the debt, while someone else made the profit?

I love to lay in bed in my jammies which usually consists of a Ninja Turtle t-shirt (I'm the Mom of five boys) and soft, cozy pants that I bought at a thrift or consignment store for a few bucks and inspire you in my writing while sipping on a great cup of coffee, mostly creamer. But while I love to relax in bed while I write my thoughts and ideas to you, I want to scream through the pages, put my hands on your face so I can grab your full attention, make you uncomfortable and make certain you are listening because this is where I have failed. Epicly. I have failed in business because of debt. I have started companies with debt, always owing someone or owing some entity. And because of the debt owed, and the debt accumulation in those companies, they never had a real chance. I failed because I was always a slave to a lender.

Why did I start a business with debt? Well, because that's what I had been taught that everyone does and everything costs money, right? Rent, utilities, payroll, taxes, unexpected expenses, inventory, lenders, credit cards, need more inventory, advertising, marketing, branding, filings, legal, etc. So we begin our business journey borrowing money and building debt. Building debt does not promise that you will build wealth. But, building debt does promise and always guarantees it builds debt. You will always have the debt and you will always have the responsibility to pay it no matter what occurs in your business. Debtors and Lenders don't care that you have a bad month or a bad year in business. They want their money.

Many home-based companies today are pushing their credit card, or pushing you into purchasing business supplies and inventory that you are pushed into thinking that you must need and must sell, so you'll need to come up with thousands of dollars in debt to purchase immediately, with no guarantees that you will sell anything! Right? That's just how they do it. And many of you have found yourselves in debt, owing a credit card company or lender for a company that does not work, or direct sales that don't really sell, closets and bathrooms full of crap, and for what? A business model that only benefits the few and certainly not you.

Enter Frugi.

I want you to start a business without going into debt. I want you to be in business where you don't have to purchase someone else's inventory to be successful. I want you to no longer or ever be a part of a pyramid scheme. I want you to change your beliefs about debt. I want you to make money.

Mic Drop. Bam!

How can you create this business? How can you do this? How can you be successful with Frugi or with your own business? No Debt. It cannot start, process or end with debt. NONE. So you will have to get serious about your finances.

You will need CASH. You will need to get organized financially. If you don't have cash, you can't start a business. You might have to wait and get it together.

Cash is key. Cash is King. Cash is how you get started. It does not matter if you need $200 or $200,000. Use Cash. When you use cash to begin, you owe no one. You make the profit. You have the flexibility to decide if you want to grow or shut it down. If your business fails, you don't feel the loss as deeply if you lose cash. But if you lose the business and then owe someone money, paying off a loan or credit and not having that business, well that just sucks and you feel pain with every payment!

Where do I find cash? Sell something. Look around you right now and see what you can sell? Whenever I organize a home or business, it's amazing how much stuff they can get rid of, sell for cash. It's amazing how much stuff they really don't use or need. It's cash just sitting there! Go without something. Stop eating and drinking out so much. Stop taking vacations you can't afford. Move to somewhere cheaper to live. Pay off your debt and see how much that opens up extra cash. Get an extra job for a few months or the holidays. I love having Garage Sales all the time! Hunker down, get it done. Earn the cash. But don't borrow it.

When you begin a business or launch your idea with cash, it just feels best! You are all in! And it's yours! You don't owe anyone or any company. Cash is the best beginning.

So, whether you are starting your Frugi Home Organizer business or starting with your own idea, start it with cash. Only after making a profit, then make payments and purchases for your business with cash. No debt. And you will never end up a slave to those lenders, that nasty interest and you can make the best decisions to grow your business to success!

NO INVENTORY

Having been a part of the Direct Sales industry, and just about every pyramid scheme that is out there, I have learned the hard way! Do you feel me? Hard way. From shakes to vitamins to veggie gummies to make-up to bags to jewelry to kitchen tools. The push is Inventory. The push is that you always need more inventory, more business supplies, more stuff! You are told and molded into believing that you must purchase inventory. Lots of it. In order to move up in the company or help someone else move up in the company and to really reach your sales goals or someone else's sales goals, purchase more inventory.

After reading one of my favorite books, "The Life-Changing Magic of Tidying Up" by Marie Kondo, using the explained Japanese art of de-cluttering and organizing, I immediately cleaned out my basement, my office, my closets, my kitchen, my pantry, my garage, my entire home. It was the most effective cleansing & organizing I had experienced in my home and I loved implementing the same concepts in my business. My Home Office became more productive, thriving, full of creative energy again! And it was truly empty. No inventory for anything. I have a table with paper, a couple pieces of electronic equipment, a file cabinet and a wall hanging white board.

Tidying up my kitchen and organizing my pantry led to a healthier lifestyle experience. I just naturally lost weight. I felt great! And there isn't a lot in my pantry. I eat fresher, healthier. Not a lot of inventory in there! And even though we are a family of seven, we don't need to stock up on everything for months of inventory, losing money on things we never eat or getting lost in the pantry chaos. It is clean, neat, organized and we make better choices when we can see it all.

Cleaning out and organizing my bathrooms, closets and storage areas was eye-opening. And it also made me really angry! I had so much product, inventory, junk, useless business items sitting for years in my bathrooms, closets, basement and garage, that had only led to debt and screwing other people to make a profit. Tidying up and getting organized made so many things in my life more clear. More certain. Knowing that I had played a part in possibly leading others into debt, or into a business model and system that only benefited a few, and realized that those companies had just flat out lied in order to make a profit off of individuals who often couldn't afford it. I could no longer play any part. There had to be a better way!

So I wanted to come up with an idea, a business model that would work in harmony with my Frugi Home Organizer business I was operating in my beautiful, small town of Parker, Co. and offer the business model to anyone who had a gift and a passion for organizing and for business! But there would be no debt, no inventory. There would be honesty, up-front costs and we would grow our businesses together. We both would make money.

Enter Frugi.

The Frugi Business Model would be No debt, No inventory, No pyramid, offer a starter kit that really gets you started, everyone would pay the same, everyone would make money, everyone would benefit from the advertising and marketing of the brand name, our Mission Statement would be clear and no fluff.

I began Frugi Home Organizer because there was low cost to start it, low risk to be involved in, no inventory of any kind needed to begin, low costs to maintain, and I love to get people organized! Now offering this business model to others is my dream come true! It's a true goal now in my life to grow my Frugi Reps because I know it is the best possibility for success in the Home-Based Business market. The best! And when a new Frugi signs up to begin his or her own business, I know this business model only allows for an environment of success, not for the success of the top producers, top sellers, the chosen few.

When thinking about and researching a company to begin with or start with, look at the inventory options. If you are currently designing your own business and reading this book in order to be best prepared for business, look at your inventory, look at the cost of the stuff. Some inventory may be necessary, but is thousands of dollars necessary? How about designing or beginning with Frugi where NO INVENTORY is necessary to get started? Feels great! Nothing to tidy or clean out or lose in the back of a closet for years! Nothing to make you angry that you went into debt or tried to sell or just filled up your home with inventory to build someone else's career. The Frugi Business Model just feels good. And if feels great offering to you!

I am thinking about starting a Frugi Home Organizer Rep business Jen, but if there is no inventory, how can I make money? Booking & organizing clients in their homes and businesses. You charge the amount for each service you offer. Cleaning, Organizing, Staging. This is the Frugi way. The only time inventory is purchased is when a client gives you a budget and authorizes you to purchase organizing tools for their home or office while you are performing your organizing work. You can choose to make a profit off of the inventory purchasing and also from your organizing work. choose the cost for your services. You make the money directly.

Let me also tell you what a No Inventory business can do. It offers you freedom! Freedom in the business market. You don't have to constantly change your price points on items to try and make a profit. You don't have to spend time making purchases and filling inventory orders for your clients and your upline and downline! No deliveries of inventory! No Inventory allows you to operate your business anywhere! You don't have to make room in your home or have a separate room for inventory. The inventory won't take over the kitchen table, ever!

Uber is a wonderful example of a No Inventory Business. Uber does not have to purchase vehicles or taxi's. No Inventory. Uber utilizes other people's cars and means of transportation to operate its business and to make a profit. If you can design a company that does not need inventory, go for it! It is also a great reason to jump on in and become a Frugi Home Organizer Rep! FrugiHomeOrganizer.com to start your business today! (Absolutely shameless and guiltless plug here because I know it can only benefit you and I am in business, you should plug the same!)

So, whether you are starting your Frugi Home Organizer business or your own business, start it with NO INVENTORY. If your business model requires an inventory, ONLY purchase it as you sell it, purchase more ONLY once it sells and you have made a profit. Pay as you grow. If at all possible, operate a Home-Based Business that does not need nor require a lot or any inventory. Just another great idea to help you be successful in any business! (Become a Frugi!)

NO PYRAMID

While envisioning the Frugi Business Model and what it would look like, feel like and operate like, trying to come up with a better system where we all make money, I was able to remember and draw upon my own personal experiences in Direct Sales & Pyramid Schemes. Having to book parties and recruit team members and go into debt to purchase inventory and ask others to do the same and having to file Bankruptcy because of all the credit card bills from inventory I had already purchased and did not sell, and having to ask my husband to cover credit card payments on months I didn't sell anything, the Direct Sales & Pyramids became even more clear to me and what I NEVER WANT TO BE AGAIN. EVER.

In business and broke.

I never want to experience a Director or National calling me to spend more money on inventory to help someone else make money (themselves) and to help someone else get a car, a jacket, a necklace, a promotion. I never want that for you.

I never want to experience again pressure of having to sell, the pressure from uplines telling me to hurry up and work harder and spend more and attend this meeting and I must go to a conference every year! UGH. I am over it! Aren't you?

I wrote down in my Frugi journal that I keep with me for my mad genius ideas, "Don't do this...." And so we don't.

At no time in any Frugi business will there be Representatives trying to become Directors, Nationals or Super-Naturals, Upline, Middlelines, Downlines. There will never be Recruits you must get, Bosses you must submit to every week, Team Members you must meet with every month, Guests and Clients that you must always try and turn into Reps, and don't get me started again on the damn inventory and on and on. Whew! That made me tired just writing all that crap!

WAKE UP! SHAKE IT UP! STOP THE CYCLE & GET OFF THE HAMSTER WHEEL! And for goodness sake, take a deep breath and open your eyes! Look around you. Is this really what you thought it would be?

Where are you in the Pyramid? The bottom crums? Driving that car yet?

How much debt are you in to drive that car? What does it cost you and your team to get a jacket or a free bag or free necklace? How much inventory do you still have because it is inventory that will never sell? Stressed out to make your numbers? Are you sick of the debt, inventory, pyramid yet?

If this system is working for you, good for you. But for the majority, it is not. You do not have to live this way. Your team members do not have to live this way. You have the power, the voice, the choice. Choose to not be a victim of the Pyramid. And just because they don't call it that, does not mean it isn't. It is a pyramid and you know it. Only the top will make money. Only the few will make a profit off of the lower levels who are left in debt and horrible financial situations. I live every day and go to sleep at night with peace knowing that Frugi is not a scheme or a pyramid scam for the benefit of only the few.

Do business and create business that is honorable, that is real, tangible and benefits ALL. No Pyramid allows for everyone the same chances, the same benefits, the same opportunities, the same growth, the same costs. Sure, some may choose to spend more, offer more, work more, and grow more. But at the base, at the core, we are the same in a No Pyramid based business model. Also, with no one above you, no one below you, we work together, we grow one another's business. If we are all the same in business ownership, there is not a team against team, there is not a stealing of recruits, there is not one person wearing a special jacket or special pin so you know they are super duper special and you aren't.

The Frugi Business Model rewards and honors your work. You make the money first. You make the money directly, not the Company, not someone above you, not someone you owe. You. No trickle-down profits. I love it! Doesn't this just feel better already!?! No schemes, no scams, nothing hidden. You make the money. This is my Frugi way. It is the only way I can offer you this business. It is the only way I can enjoy my amazing life and sleep in peace. It is how I choose to run and operate businesses. And it feels amazing! You should try it! You are making money, I make money and it is a win-win for all. And we have some fun too! We celebrate our successes! We party! We love life together! We support one another!

I know this may have offended you. I know you may be wrapped up in a pyramid or direct sales company right now, so this just won't make sense to you. It will hurt your feelings that I am calling it bull****! It is wrong to help people go into debt. Think about that. It is wrong to make gain only for your benefit and act like it benefits others. Don't act like helping people into debt is not your responsibility. "Well, they didn't have to buy all that inventory", but you helped them. "Well, they want to go after the same goals and I'm the only one who did it right", then it was your responsibility to show them how. "Well, they wanted that stuff they really couldn't afford", that was your sale. "Well, they knew what they were getting into", and now we are supposed to feel good about that? Can you see or visualize the sickness in the pyramid system at all?

Frugi has a head. That's me. And then we have some other heads who care for our H.R., Accounting, Legal, Advertising & Marketing the Brand, Administration, Booking Agent & so on. Unlike a Pyramid where only the heads would make the money, in a Frugi Business Model, it's the opposite. From the bottom up, Reps make the money. The heads all get paid, but only after money is produced and deposited. So, instead of a regular pyramid model where money is first placed with the company, where then the company takes a huge portion then trickles it down to the lowest levels, Frugi allows the lowest level to make the money and then a smaller portion is paid up directly to the Company. This is how we stop the Pyramid. This is how Reps make the most money, not just the company.

So, whether you are starting your Frugi Home Organizer business or your own new business concept, think of business as a Circle, not a Pyramid. Money for all, not just for some. Always be thinking about how you and others can make money together. It is amazing what it will do for your business culture, atmosphere, growth and passion for everyone's success!

A STARTER KIT THAT REALLY GETS YOU STARTED

So excited! It's coming today! My first Starter Kit for my first Direct Sales company! So excited to get started and start selling and making money! And then it arrives! My wonderful UPS driver leaves it on the front porch. Something this amazing cannot be left on the porch! It must be opened and unraveled and relished immediately! And then I opened it.

That's it? That's all? How do I start a business with this? It is as depressing as the moment in the movie, The Christmas Story, when the main character is so excited to unlock the code to a game prize he has been working so hard to find the letters from a radio show he listens to every night, only to find when he spells out the letters, it is a commercial, a stupid ad to drink his chocolate milk.

I get it buddy! Been there! More than a few times! Call me crazy, I just kept trying those companies and hoping their Starter Kit would be better than the previous one. Crazy. Or is this the perfect definition for insanity? Silly me. I forgot that the "Starter Kit" was truly just a bag, a couple pieces of inspirational papers, a keychain maybe, possibly a pen with logo, and instructions on how to order everything I would need to be successful at this current business. The instructions read that I would need to order all of my business supplies and then order all of my inventory to really get started. A Starter Kit that really didn't get me started.

Enter Frugi.

If I was going to offer Frugi to the masses, or just to my best friend or neighbor, I was going to need to design a Starter Kit that really gets people started in their business on the first day. So our Business Model is such. When you order your Starter Kit from us, it includes everything you will need to begin your business with nothing else needed to purchase or invest in. Crazy! Frugi Home Organizer sends you Personalized Business Cards, Personalized Car Vehicle Decal, Logo Business Bag, Logo Work Shirt, Marketing Postcards. These items are ordered only after a new Frugi Rep pays for them. So there is NO INVENTORY. These items are sent directly to the new Frugi Rep as they are made, personalized, printed, and shipped. It is how we keep the costs down for the items and this is what you need to start your business with Frugi.

If you are preparing another business idea, have a concept or are looking to help others get started, keep it simple, keep it real and honest, and when you say you are giving them a "Starter" Kit, really give them a Starter Kit. This is the Frugi Business Model. A Starter Kit that really gets you started. You will have your business cards to hand out, Postcards to mail out, Car Decal to advertise you wherever you go, and a Logo work shirt and Logo bag to look the part and advertise your business while working and networking, or just doing gardening.

Now you can get excited! You can get excited many times! Since all the items are shipped separately and come in separate packages at different times, you get to enjoy the experience of excitement many times over! Remember, nothing else to buy. You are in business. Get started!

Does Frugi make money from the Starter Kit? Yes. I pay myself a salary from anything Frugi produces, and then I advertise us and grow our brand to help you grow your business. The Starter Kit helps to pay for company salaries, administrative & advertising costs, plus the cost to make the kit items and get them to you. A Frugi Starter Kit, or "Fresh Start", costs a little bit more than other Home-Based Direct Sales market companies because Frugi never asks you for additional funds to get your business started and we aren't directly selling anything except our services. We don't ask you to buy more business stuff, we don't ask you to buy thousands in inventory, we don't hammer you with costs for web pages, merchandise, meetings, Facebook Ads, etc. Frugi does the advertising, marketing, webpage, mobile app, conferences, training sessions, and pays legal fees to protect our company and brand. There are a lot of costs associated with

Frugi, so we all share in the cost and we all share in the paying and we all share in the growing.

How do you know this is all I need to begin my business? Because I have started many businesses and worked for many companies. I have started retail from the ground up, I've started Direct Sales, I've started online business, I've started enough companies to get it. I know what my own Frugi Home Organizer business needed in the beginning and I know what you need now. I have already gone through the experience for you! I have failed at business and have been successful. I know what it takes, and what it doesn't.

Why would I sign up to become a Frugi Home Organizer Representative when I can just start my own Home-Based Organizing business? Right?! Yes! You Can! Go for it! If this is truly your passion, your desire to start your own business and not be associated with anyone else, that is fabulous! Take the information from this book and run with it! Go be successful! I would love to hear about your endeavor and encourage you!

What I have found in my 20 plus years of business is that a Brand Name is crucial and Advertising is even more crucial to the success of any business. What I also have found is that being in business is freaking hard! There is a lot to do as a Small Business Owner! Especially when we are starting out! Frugi does a lot of business for you. Just like owning a franchise, we continue to build brand and name recognition and continue to create advertising campaigns that benefit our reps and our company mission. Frugi does the side of business that you don't want to or have time for. You can spend your time building your client base and growing your organizing business while we do the other side of business that you might really not want to spend the time doing. Advertising is expensive. Campaigns are extremely expensive. Networking is time consuming. Organizing is time consuming. So focus on what you need to be doing and let us focus on what we can be doing for you. This is why you should sign up with Frugi! We've got you covered! You can be the first Frugi and the only Frugi in your area for years! We are new, we are growing, and branding takes years to develop and succeed maximum exposure and recognition. And when we do? Watch it POP!

My hope for you is success! No matter if you become a Frugi or head out on your own. (Become a Frugi today!) FrugiHomeOrganizer.com

So, when you begin your Frugi career, you will know that you are getting a true Starter Kit that starts your business at an extremely low cost. If you begin another business, know what your Start-Up costs will be. Set your starting budget and stay within budget. How you begin your business often determines how it succeeds or how it ends.

A MISSION STATEMENT THAT WORKS

Frugi Home Organizer, LLC. Mission Statement:

We are going to make money and live debt free
By helping others get organized and live burden free
So that all of us can be successful and live completely free.

Why is a Mission Statement so important? It sets the tone. It sets the goals. It sets the atmosphere throughout your organization and within your team. It sets everything in motion and assists in keeping the motion moving forward. Many companies write extraordinary Mission Statements, I mean really fabulous words. They spend hundreds if not thousands to have someone come up with some catchy sayings and fluffy words that make us feel….. fluffy.

I wrote Frugi Home Organizer Mission Statement with no fluff in mind, just you and me and my family and your family. That's it. And I am very honest as to what you and I are going to do. You and I are going to make money if we work our asses off. You and I are going to live debt free. We will both do this by helping people get organized which removes so many burdens from their lives and we will do this together so that we all can be successful in business and in life. Living "completely free" will have many different meanings to all of you. For me personally, "completely free" means never having to rely on a lender, or someone else to pay my bills. It means I can vacation after working hard wherever I want to and drive whatever car I want to and make my home beautiful. "Completely free" to me means only being surrounded by the people, the work and the things that I love. Eating at wonderful restaurants, traveling with family and friends, and being able to give freely to those in need at any time.

What does "completely free" mean to you?

Maybe this becomes your Mission Statement?

What is important to you? Being debt free and helping you live debt free is important to me. It's the first line. Helping others through organizing and taking others burdens from them, off their lists and shoulders. Second line. I love doing this! Every day! Another thing that I am completely sold out, passionate, crazy about??? Being successful in our businesses! Being successful in our journey, our lives, our loves! Success feels so amazing! I want that for you! When we live debt free, burden free, we can be completely free. Third line.

Write your Mission Statement for your business, for your life. Even when you become a Frugi, write your own Mission Statement for your personal business. This is your dream, your goals, your path. And then lean in, take steps, and push forward to live your mission. Aren't you excited to get started right now? I mean come on! I am giving you my best here! This is really good stuff, you should use it.

While I have you for only a few remaining moments, of course I want to attract you to my tribe of Frugi's and I want to share with you all the benefits of using the Frugi Business Model and I want to remind you of why you need to be in business with no debt, no inventory, and no pyramid. But truly, really, I want to speak directly to your soul.

If you will allow me the honor of a few more minutes of your time.

My life is not perfect. But it is perfectly my life. I love it just the way it is. I have experienced deep loss in a marriage that failed and in my relationships with my parents whom I haven't spoken to in years. I have experienced deep loss in my businesses and my ventures. I have been experienced great loss in being bankrupt and I have owed massive debt. I have experienced deep loss in the death of my precious sister too young which forever changed my present and my future. I have experienced adopting a son who may never connect to me. I have experienced losing friendships, losing jobs, just flat out losing. I have experienced incredible disappointment in the church, in people who claim to love God, and experienced the pure evil of wicked people who wanted to harm me and my family. I have failed financially, physically, emotionally and spiritually. I have failed my husband. I have failed my children. I have lost, I have failed. Can you relate to any of that?

I do love my life just the way it is. I have designed it, and it has designed me. Because all the loss, all of my experiences, all of the failures have made me exactly who I am today and have created amazing success in my life! I have been married to an amazing husband now for over 12 years. We have five great kids together. We have been through hell and back and he is the one I want to be with. Forever. I still don't speak to my parents and it opened up a world to me of others who have Mommy & Daddy issues. People who do not love you unconditionally can't be in your life anyway and it has made me a better parent, a better person. My businesses are flourishing, thriving, blessed. I am no longer a slave to lenders and live in financial freedom never experienced before! I miss my sister every day and I live my best life for her! My adoptive son lives on his own now, doing great! And invites us into his world when he is ready. And I love every minute! I still don't attend a church, but I have the best relationship with God I've ever had once I left it. Evil people still exist. But we move on and live the best life in our existence.

I have scars on my heart that will only be healed in heaven. My scars make me who I am. My scars and fine lines on my face make me unique. Make me.

It does not matter what any person or any entity has ever done to you. We all have mommy issues. We all have daddy issues. We have experienced loss. We all have experienced great loss. But, you know what is so great about life and its design? It gives us the ability to rise up, to move on, to live again, to reinvent, to become new.

I have the most amazing life! I love life! I am thrilled to wake up every morning and see the world of possibilities and what I will create! I am doing my best and being my best and living my best life! And living simply. Simply living my life. "Frugi" is a Latin term for "Frugal". Living Frugal does not mean you have to live without, live in horrid conditions, and be cheap. Living Frugi means you live with only what you need and what you love. Simply. It's how I live and that's how I run my business.

I am so excited for the next chapter in your life! What will it read? Will you become a Frugi Home Organizer and become a part of a tribe that loves you and wants to grow with you? Will you start your very own next big thing from Home? Will you begin the journey to become your best?

Whatever your next move, please take the Frugi Business Model and place it in your start-up business. Take pieces, take it whole. But take it! I know it will produce a firm foundation for your business. A Home-Based Business can be started simply and be successful. Let's begin!

ABOUT THE AUTHOR

Jennifer Chase

Mother of five boys.
Married to Dan Chase.
Lives in beautiful Colorado.
Entrepreneur.
Loves coffee & sushi.
Living Frugi.
Mad Genius.
Planning the next big thing.

@FrugiLife

FrugiHomeOrganizer.com

Look for the next book!

Simple Success

**How to Build a Successful Home-Based Business.
Simply.**

www.ingramcontent.com/pod-product-compliance
Lightning Source LLC
Chambersburg PA
CBHW070311190526
45169CB00004B/1580